Pamela M Nievas

My Mummy Milkies

A JOURNEY THROUGH BREASTFEEDING

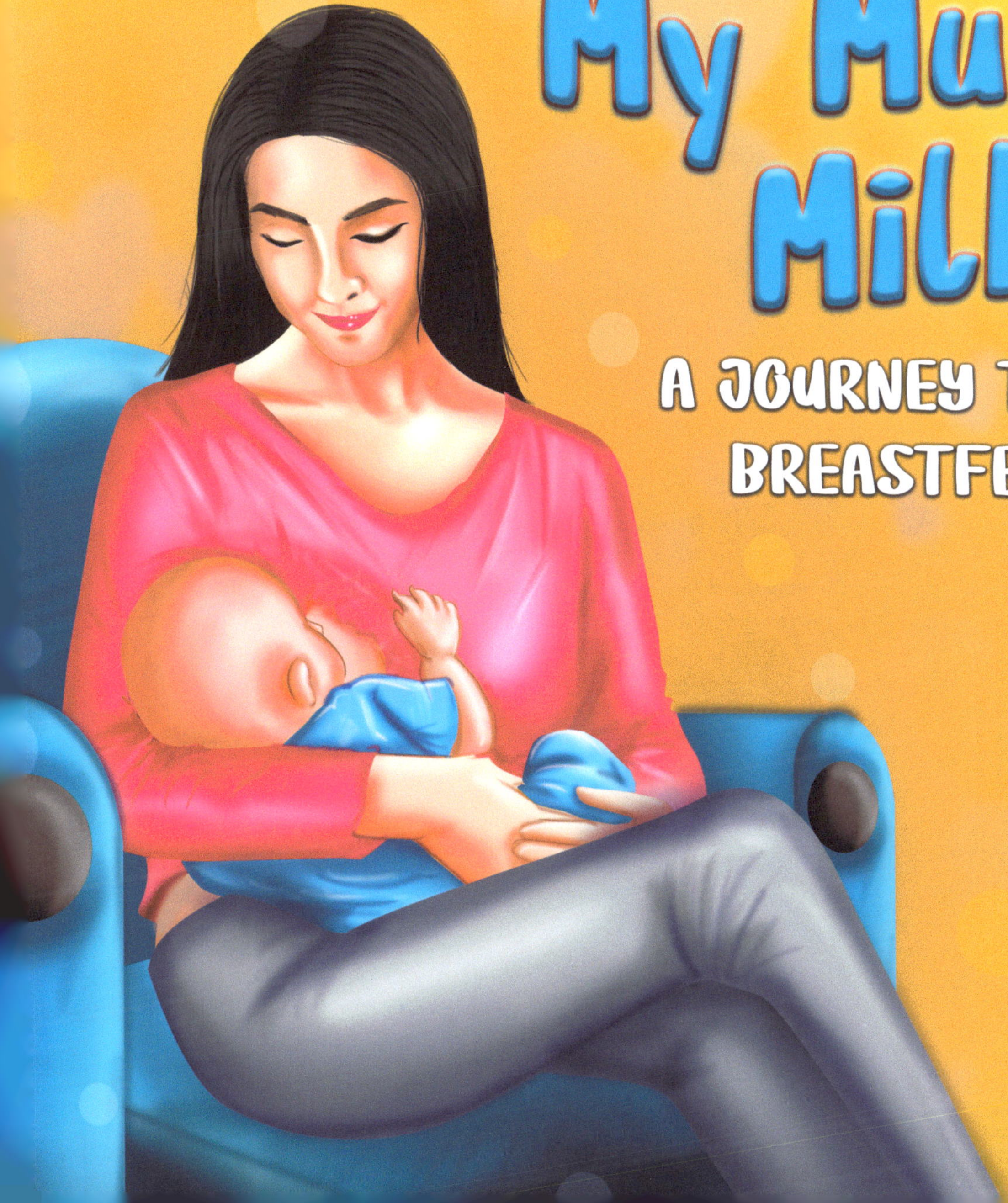

My Mummy Milkies
Copyright © 2020 by Pamela M Nievas

All rights reserved. No part of this publication may be reproduced, distributed, or transmitted in any form or by any means, including photocopying, recording, or other electronic or mechanical methods, without the prior written permission of the author, except in the case of brief quotations embodied in critical reviews and certain other non-commercial uses permitted by copyright law.

Tellwell Talent
www.tellwell.ca

ISBN
978-0-2288-4275-0 (Hardcover)
978-0-2288-4274-3 (Paperback)
978-0-2288-4276-7 (eBook)

Dedication

I would like to take this opportunity to thank my awesome family and friends for their constant support throughout the process of this book and throughout my entire life. In particular, I am thankful to my loving husband George, my darling children Valentino and Ruby, my mother Rosa, my father Victor, my niece Alyssa, and my siblings Vanesa and Alejandro.

Acknowledgement

This book is to acknowledge mothers and encourage them to not be afraid to breastfeed their children anywhere they go. You are doing an amazing job, and nothing beats the bond created through breastfeeding.

Draw or write a lasting message on this page for you and your mummy:

My mummy holds me close when I have my milkies and I love it because...

...drinking milkies makes me big and strong.

I have my mummy milkies when I am happy, hungry, sick, sad, and sleepy.

I have my mummy milkies...

...at the park when I need a rest from playing so much...

...at the beach when I've spent all day making sand castles, collecting seashells, and swimming in the water...

...at my Nonna and Nonno's house while visiting and singing songs...

...at play group when I get to see all my friends...

...at the shopping centre while buying yummy food to cook...

...at the local café where my mummy talks to her friends and they see how funny I am...

...on the way home when we wait for our train to arrive at the station...

...and even on the plane when we go on fun holidays.

When it's time to celebrate my birthday, I have my milkies while gazing into my mummy's eyes. I taste the sweet milk that makes my tummy warm and fuzzy. I touch my mummy's soft skin and smooth hair. I smell the cookies and buttercake my mummy spent all day baking. I hear my friends playing and having fun. It's just me and my mummy, and I know she does all this for me. I feel so loved.

When we get home from our adventures, and it's time for bed, my mummy reads me my favourite bedtime book.

After my bedtime book, I love my milkies because they keep me warm and safe at night. But most of all I love my milkies because they keep my mummy close and I love my mummy very much.

Thank you, Mummy;
you are always there for me.

Epilogue

My Mummy Milkies is a bedtime story depicting the breastfeeding journey of a child through different scenarios. As the child explores the world, Pamela Nievas captures the heartwarming bond a mother has with their child through breastfeeding wherever they go, whether it be at a café, at a public place, or on a mode of transport. The use of different ethnicities is embraced throughout the book to normalize breastfeeding in all aspects.

About the Author

 Pamela Nievas (also known as Pamela Novo) is a talented educator who loves spending time with her husband and two young children. After being awarded a Westpac Scholarship for Young Technologist, Pamela was soon named and featured in the Westpac *200 Women: who will change the way you see the world* book that showcases powerful and influential women with different perspectives on society.

Her children became the inspiration for *My Mummy Milkies* as she has had the privilege to experience the highs and lows of breastfeeding long term and is still breastfeeding to this day. Pamela believes all mothers who choose to breastfeed should be made to feel comfortable wherever they go. Support her Facebook page via https://fb.me/PamelaNievasMMM.

www.ingramcontent.com/pod-product-compliance
Lightning Source LLC
LaVergne TN
LVHW071651060526
838200LV00029B/425